HOROSCOPES FOR DOGS

HOROSCOPES FOR DOGS

by Jeane Dixon

illustrated by L. Mason Williams

HOUGHTON MIFFLIN COMPANY BOSTON

1979

Library of Congress Cataloging in Publication Data
Dixon, Jeane.   Horoscopes for dogs.
1. Horoscopes. 2. Dogs. I. Title.
BF1728.3.D59   133.5′8′6367   78-26868
ISBN 0-395-27453-2

Printed in the United States of America

T 10 9 8 7 6 5 4 3 2 1

This book is dedicated to
Catherine Briggs and Ruby Brown.

Through their love and caring for animals, and
their concern for people, they have made
Peace Plantation in Virginia
a haven of joy and kindness and a refuge for
all of God's creatures.
What a magnificent reality, knowing people
who care!

CONTENTS

INTRODUCTION

Every dog has his day, says the old adage. And now, his own horoscope too!

This little book is about the animals that have the biggest place in our hearts: our dogs — little or large, plain or fancy, pups or old faithfuls. It is for all animal lovers, but especially dog lovers, including every boy or girl who was ever followed home by some strange pooch. If we think back a bit we will doubtless recall that we were one of those youngsters.

But horoscopes for dogs? Certainly! Why not? They come into this world under the same stars as we do and live out their loving lives under the same astral influences as their masters.

Some people may not have accurate records of their pets' birthdays, so it may be necessary for them to approximate that date of birth and the consequent astrological sign. For example, if you received a puppy for Christmas and it was about a month old at the time, you can carefully compare your pet's personality with those described in the chapters for both Capricorn and Sagittarius, or even Scorpio a little earlier, just in case the pet store was somewhat vague about the pup's exact age.

I am sure, however, that dog owners will want to read all of these chapters — after reading their own pet's horoscope first, of course. For there is not a dog in the world, ours or someone else's, that does not enrich people's lives in some way — with a joyous bark, perhaps, or with the warm, searching eyes of a quiet companion.

So it has been from the beginning, ever since that first scraggly dog abandoned life in the wild to become domesticated and share man's food and man's future. Crouching low to the ground, hiding behind a rock or tree on some starry night long ago, the nameless animal watched the human figures gathered around mysterious flames, which lit up the night and cast eerie shadows. What strange noises they made—much more complicated than canine speech—and sometimes they broke into a kind of music called song.

There were little humans with them—boys and girls. But all were as frisky as pups. They certainly seemed harmless enough, if the dog only dared to make their acquaintance.

I cannot say for sure, but I like to believe that, then as now, it was probably one of those primitive youngsters who brought home the first dog, saying to Mom and Dad, "He followed me. Can we keep him?"

We can imagine the parents' reactions as the child approached the campfire in the night with the wary animal—half frightened, half hopeful—following a few steps behind, wondering what the adults would do when they saw him. Perhaps they rushed for their weapons and snatched up the child to save it from the beast. And only when the dog did not run away, but looked up at them through eyes glowing with friendliness, did they realize that their little one had brought them a new companion.

Thus did mankind find a willing servant, a trusty guardian, and a sturdy worker. But most of all, a pet, a playmate, a pal. By establishing its own relationship with mankind, the dog taught humans to appreciate animals and to see in them admirable

characteristics. That is something we are still learning, as we discover the many ways we and animals depend upon one another for our common survival.

But there is much more to be learned about our most familiar pets. Whatever their breed—or mixture of breeds—just as we do, they reflect a rainbow of personalities just as we do, which, all together, comprise the zodiac. To someone who has never been so fortunate as to have a dog, that may come as a surprise. But to anyone who has had a pooch in the house, there is just no denying that our canine friends are as distinctively intriguing as any human member of the family.

This is *their* book, and how I wish they could read it! We can imagine the conversation among the dogs in our own neighborhood: "Well, I'm a Libra, but I especially liked what Jeane had to say about Virgo." "My cousin, the Doberman, says he's an Aries; but I see a lot of Gemini in him."

But that is wishful thinking. And anyway, our dogs do not need horoscopes to tell them that their happiness depends upon living in harmony with their stars and with their favorite humans. *That* they understand by instinct. But perhaps we people can find in this little book the insights we need into our pets' personalities. That way, we can do our part to continue the wonderful partnership begun, many thousands of years ago, by the little child who brought the first dog to his family's campfire somewhere in the dark of night, under the twinkling stars.

ARIES

Dogs born under the sign of the astral Ram have the same personality traits as Aries people: They are headstrong and impulsive. When they want to run across the neighbor's lawn, they trample the KEEP OFF THE GRASS signs. When they hear the bell of the ice-cream wagon, they jump the fence to chase after their favorite delicacy.

A wise owner of an Aries puppy will begin early to direct its enthusiasm into the right channels by teaching it that there are times for impetuous behavior and other times for calm obedience. Your Aries pup is a diamond in the rough, and all it takes is a little polishing to have one of the real gems of the animal kingdom.

Like his cousins under the sign of Leo, the Aries dog is a natural leader. In a race, he is the front runner. In a canine argument (these things do happen, even with the best of dogs) he is the likely winner. When it is time for his dinner, he will rush you over to the closet where his food is kept, trying to show you where it is—just in case you have forgotten. When it is time for his walk, nothing else can interrupt. And if you should have an emergency telephone call at that same time, he will bark his protests into the receiver.

You will probably overlook these exuberant and headstrong

13

habits because they are all part of a package that you cannot help but love. Your pet will learn quickly and will readily admit his mistakes. When he must be punished—very gently punished, of course, which is the only way any pet should be chastised—he will understand his mistake and rarely will he repeat it.

An Aries pooch readily accepts responsibilities. He loves to be put in charge. If it is his job to guard the house, or patrol the yard, or play lifeguard at the beach, he feels on top of the world. His sense of duty is tremendous. That is why a large Aries dog makes a terrific watch dog, once he has overcome his impulsive ways. He could also be a prized sheep dog, herding his wayward flock to its destination, while fiercely defending against predators.

Your Aries pet is tenacious. When he feels he is right, he will not give up easily. That is why you must learn to respect his rights, just as you want him to respect yours. It is important not to bother him while he is eating, just as you would not want him to take your plate away during dinner. And when he feels like a snooze, give him his well-earned rest. Like an Aries person, your dog does not demand much; but the few things he insists upon are essential to him.

An unusual aspect of Ariens is that, in their youth, they frequently come under the influence of a friend or teacher who changes their lives for the better by setting them on the road to greatness. This is true of dogs as well as people. For your pet, you may be that inspiring teacher and encouraging friend. Your patient guidance and care may transform your Aries pooch into a champion show dog, an outstanding performer, or a remarkably intelligent member of your household. Always remember that your dog's future is not just in the stars. It is also in your hands.

TAURUS

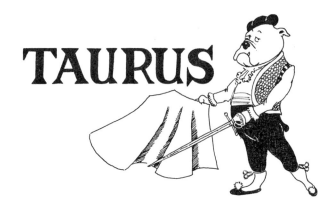

Dogs born under the sign of Taurus share the qualities of the astral bull: strength, courage, endurance, determination, pride, and enthusiasm. What a powerful personality! So, they can be a little hard to handle, especially by someone who does not appreciate their admirable virtues. Or they can be affectionate whirlwinds, bringing joy to their owners with their outbursts of fun-filled energy.

Your Taurus pet does not have to be a bulldog. A stately Afghan or a tiny Shih Tzu can still reflect the bullish traits that make a Taurus one of the dynamos of the animal kingdom.

Taurus dogs are prized for their physical stamina. They gladly pull sleds through Arctic snows and accompany troops on cross-country hikes. Given a task, they stick to it. This makes them eager performers when their masters teach them tricks, and the applause of an audience warms their proud Taurean hearts.

Their inborn bravery makes them daredevils, and they sometimes take risks too lightly. For the average household pet, this Taurean courage can cause problems, especially with traffic. By teaching your puppy to stay out of the street, you will spare him possible trouble later on.

The determination that makes a Taurus dog a reliable worker can also make him stubborn. He can be pushed only so far. Sometimes he will break his leash rather than give up his plans for a walk. He likes to follow his usual routine and may become unhappy when his food dish is in the wrong place or he is expected to sleep in a strange room. An understanding master will reassure his confused pet with lively conversation and warm smiles.

Because Taurus dogs, like Taurus people, are proud, special care should be taken not to hurt their feelings. Your pet should not be punished in front of strangers or other dogs. When you must scold him, be sure to make up soon afterward, for nothing hurts a Taurus more than angry words.

Taurus is a bull with a lamb's heart. There is a tremendous tenderness within these forceful animals. They are the romping Irish setter who gently plays with the new kittens in the neighborhood, or the ponderous Old English sheepdog who can carry a lost chick back to its nest without hurting it. Their kindness knows no bounds, until someone mistreats them. Then they can be as fierce as the charging *toro* of the bull ring.

The heroic qualities of Taurus make him a vigorous competitor. Even as a pup, he loves to join children in rough-and-tumble sports. In autumn, when the kids play football, he thinks he is a champion tackle and insists upon joining the game. In summer, he plays the outfield and runs away with the baseball.

It is in times of trouble that Taurus is at his champion best. Then he is reliable and sympathetic. Sensing when his master is worried, he will take his doggie playthings to him to cheer him up. His exuberant love of life seems to drive away sadness from his family. Boisterous Taurus brings his own sunshine into the lives of his human friends.

GEMINI

Gemini is the Latin word for twins, and those born under this sign—pups and people alike—reflect the two-sided nature of the starry Twins. They are great talkers with very definite opinions, so your Gemini pet may bark a bit more than most other dogs. They are true charmers. Every time you take your Gemini pooch out for a walk, passers-by compliment your handsome companion.

Geminis are intelligent and busy, always alert and ready for action. They are versatile and adaptable, ready to take on any new game. They would equally enjoy vacationing with their owners in the mountains or at the seashore. Most of all, they like surprises and unexpected changes. They enjoy something unusual for dinner now and then, and often like to sleep in different rooms on different nights. This makes your Gemini pet unpredictable, and you probably wonder where she learned her new trick or picked up her latest habit. That is part of her charm, and it keeps your pet always interesting and young in spirit.

There is, however, another side to these personality traits. You may have already noticed it in your Gemini dog. Her inquisitive nature can make her nosy. This can be a bother when she absolutely insists

upon personally inspecting everything in the house or in a neighbor's yard. Her changeability can make her restless and fickle. Yesterday's favorite toy is ignored today. Her taste for new experiences and different environments may even lead her to run away from home, and when you track her down a few blocks away, enjoying the hospitality of the new family in the community, she will not be the least bit repentant. She just likes to meet new folks!

Like human Geminis, animals born under the sign of the Twins do not like confining relationships. They resist being tied down to one spot or to one person. Part of their charm is that they make friends quickly, but this also means that their affections are spread around to many people. They need a social environment, with new people coming and going. That is why they often like to visit schoolyards, where there are dozens of children to frolic with. They are at their best during a family reunion, going from person to person to inspect the visitors and to seek out interesting or amusing guests.

A Gemini dog is as enjoyable as a three-ring circus. She is always involved in something new. But that means she probably does not handle routine matters very well. She is long on cleverness and short on responsibility. But your Gemini pet was not born to perform guard duty or fetch and carry. We all have our different roles to play in life, and hers is to enliven the world with her frisky personality and delightful ways.

CANCER

If your dog loves to play in water, howl at the moon, and protect your home from strangers—including the mailman and delivery boys—then chances are your pet was born under the sign of the crab or, to use its fancy Latin name, the sign of Cancer. Like humans born under the sign of the crab, Cancerian dogs love the ocean. Most are born swimmers, even though they may hate to take a bath. They especially like to stroll along the banks of a stream or along the beach, where they can pretend to be lifeguards, keeping an eye out for catfish!

A Cancerian dog is shrewd and cautious, and that is why your pet is often reluctant to explore new walkways and hiding places. He likes to thoroughly sniff over new acquaintances before deciding if they are friend or foe. This makes him a great watchdog, sometimes too much so! He may go overboard in defending his master's house, not even letting relatives come in without his barking and growling to let them know this home is under his protection.

Every once in a while, a Cancerian pooch likes some time to himself. Cancerian people often meditate alone to collect their thoughts and refresh their spirits, and pets born under the same star

sign behave the same way. If they do not meditate, they at least relax and refresh their psychic energy. So if your Cancer pup sometimes sits by himself and does not want to play, let him have his peaceful moments at rest. He will soon come romping back to see what you are up to.

No animal is more faithful than a Cancerian dog. To those who love him, he returns his total devotion. He will protect them even at great danger to himself. And he is well equipped for that job because, under the influence of the moon, he is sensitive and alert. He can hear someone approaching the house even before the door-bell rings, and he can smell smoke when it is only a tiny ash.

Most Cancer dogs are humble. They rarely win first prize in dog shows because they would prefer to stay at home with their family rather than strut around for the judges.

But there are more important things than winning blue ribbons. If your pet is a Cancerian, you already know what I mean; for you have a faithful friend who wants, most of all, to protect his loved ones and serve their every need.

LEO

A dog born under the sign of Leo possesses many of the qualities of that noble Lion. He is a born leader, always out in front of the pack. When you are out for a walk together, he likes to run in front of you, sometimes endangering himself with his recklessness.

Even though he is lovable, he does have a temper. When he is angry, he will snap and snarl. But he is also the most forgiving of creatures, quick to make up and ready to overlook an offense as soon as the offender wants to be friends again. A Leo dog who has been mistreated does not hold grudges. He will, however, insist upon being respected and treated fairly. Otherwise, he will either run away or defend himself.

That is why a Leo should have a strong, but loving, master who can appreciate all the wonderful qualities of a leonine pet. Your dog is warm and generous. When he welcomes you home, the whole world knows you have arrived. His barking and racing around the room are a better greeting than an entire marching band!

He is also impulsive and powerful. Even a little Leo, a toy poodle or a Scottie, is stronger than you would expect and is always dashing off with the suddenness of a jack-in-the-box. A walk in the woods

with him is an unforgettable experience. Without any warning, he is off and racing after a rabbit or running through the leaves just for fun.

Leo dogs are compulsive workers. They just cannot stop doing things. They will dig all day in the garden if you let them; and when you play tug of war with them, they want the game to last forever. If you teach your pet to fetch a stick, he will soon fill up the yard with twigs. And some surprised pet owners have found that their Leo pooch brought them several newspapers—their own and the neighbors' too!

Leo dogs are basically tolerant. They like to live and let live. Oh, they will chase cats, but they do not go out of their way to find trouble. They instinctively search for the good in any situation, staying on the sunny side of life.

They are, however, theatrical. They love to show off. This is their way of asking you for a compliment and a pat on the head. Perhaps you have tried to teach a Leo puppy to roll over and he began to tumble all around the room. That's Leo for you: always overdoing things.

This is usually a good characteristic, especially when a Leo dog is fortunate enough to have an owner who shares his zest for living and who returns his total loyalty. Like the people who share their star sign, Leo pets usually have a happy home life. But it is up to their masters to make sure of that.

So if your dog is a Leo, remember that your energetic friend needs ample food, cool water, and plenty of exercise to maintain his lionlike spirit. Remember, too, that his faithful affection will be yours as long as you show him you appreciate it with your kindness.

VIRGO

Whether a person or pooch, a Virgo is sensitive and refined, enjoying the beautiful things of nature. Your Virgo pet may sometimes sniff at the flowers in your garden or lie quietly at your feet while you are listening to music. She likes it too!

A Virgo dog can be as observant as the best art critic, as discriminating as a gourmet, and as meticulous as a diamond cutter. Even a Virgo Great Dane or Doberman will eat daintily, rarely upsetting her water dish. Like their human counterparts, Virgo pooches are blessed with good memories. They seldom forget where they have buried their bones and sometimes find their way home over long distances all by themselves.

Because a Virgo dog is painstaking and careful, she is well equipped to be trained for all sorts of demanding tasks, especially as a guide for the blind or as a pathfinder in the wilderness.

Virgo people demand a clean and healthy environment, and Virgo pets are no different. Your Virgo dog cannot be happy if she has to sleep in a neglected doghouse or in a cluttered cellar, or if you fail to keep her washed and groomed. For some other dogs, having tangled hair and muddy paws would be only a nuisance; but for

Virgos, it is a disaster. It can affect their health and change their whole attitude toward life. So from the time you first welcome a Virgo puppy into your home, until it reaches a ripe old age of Virgoan wisdom, be sure to give your pet the same kind of attention you would want for yourself if you were born under the sign of the Lady of the Stars.

Because Virgo pets are endowed with refined senses, they observe things which other animals would overlook. That is why they occasionally search through the house, sniffing out the source of some minor scent which no one else has noticed. The perfect job as a working Virgo would be as the guard dog in an art museum. She could wander from room to room all night, basking in the quiet glow of the beautiful masterpieces and using her acute senses to detect any threat from fire or burglary.

Like a human Virgo, a Virgo dog intuitively feels when someone is sick or unhappy. It is not unusual for a Virgo to mope around when her human is ill. Somehow, the dog always seems to know when her friends are worried or sad. At those times, she will be especially quiet, remaining near her owner, to listen to his troubles or to lick away a tear.

If you own a Virgo pet, you are familiar with the pattern that you can count on your faithful friend in good times and bad. Just remember to give her the attention Virgos love, with the clean and wholesome surroundings Virgos need. And if she sometimes nibbles on your favorite flowers, that will be a small price to pay for having such a gentle and genuine friend.

LIBRA

The main characteristic of Libra dogs and Libra people is a sense of balance in all things. Whether your Libra is a mighty Great Dane or a tiny Chihuahua, he is not likely to knock over household objects. He is never lazy but, on the other hand, never runs himself into exhaustion. He takes the middle path through life, and it is rare to see a Libra doggie who is either overweight or skinny, unless his master has neglected him.

Even Libra puppies have exceptional poise. They do not often get themselves tripped up in their own feet and tails, as most pups do.

Just like Libra people, the Libra dog is curious and inquisitive. He is always exploring some corner of the house or garden, or nosing around underneath tables and in closets. He loves to watch other animals at play but rarely quarrels with them. In fact, he will usually back down from a growling fight. With people, too, he avoids conflict and stays on his best behavior so he will not annoy or disappoint his master.

A Libra pooch has a strong sense of duty. He will risk his life to save his human friends and would never damage property while roaming around the neighborhood. Because he is so very responsi-

ble, he can often be trusted to guard little children and to protect the home from strangers.

An atmosphere of harmony is essential for the health and happiness of a Libra dog. If his owners are quarrelsome and nervous, then their Libra pet, sensing the discord around him, may even run away from home in order to escape it. If his owners have an unhappy marriage, he will suffer from it as much as they because he will sense their tension.

All Libra dogs have high personal standards. They are not likely to roll in mud puddles or track up a clean kitchen floor.

Because they are usually so obedient, their owners often have a reputation for being wonderful pet trainers. The Libra doggie, mild and faithful, does not mind if his master gets all the credit. All he asks in return is a balanced diet, an even-handed disposition, and a peaceful home.

SCORPIO

Scorpio is the sign of intense, passionate, and hardy people—or dogs, as the case may be. A canine born under the influence of the starry Scorpion shares with human Scorpios one of the strongest, liveliest, and most exciting personalities in the entire zodiac.

The first time you hug your Scorpio puppy, you notice its forceful spirit. When it is happy, it will throw the whole house into a jumble with its playfulness. When it is sad or lonely at night, it will keep everyone—including the neighbors—awake with its crying. It must be raised with both firmness and gentleness in order to restrain its Scorpio ardor while nurturing its Scorpio dynamism.

Once your pet has been taught to discipline his feelings, he is a prince among canines. His heart is full of passion. He loves life and worships his master. His sharp wits make him a cunning hunter and an engaging playmate. You cannot hide a thing from this alert fellow. He is always on his guard, even when he seems most relaxed. Woe to the trespasser who breaks into the home of a Scorpio watchdog!

Whether a pedigree or a mutt, a Scorpio dog is rugged and adaptable. Even if he looks small and scrawny, his nerves are steely

and his determination is immense. He can survive against great odds in Arctic snows or in desert wastelands. His attitude is the canine version of "the power of positive thinking." He is the buoyant optimist, ready to do the impossible. He will keep trying to jump a troublesome fence until he clears it, and he will pester you for a second helping of dinner until you give in.

Scorpio dogs are tremendous achievers. They set their sights high, especially when their owners encourage them to excel. With a dedicated master, they can be champion racers, proud show dogs, or masterful hunters. Or they can be something even more important: the most enthusiastic and energetic dogs in their neighborhoods.

But there is another side to all these traits: Scorpios are pivotal characters, which means they can abruptly change course and veer off in the opposite direction. If they are neglected by their owners, their intensity can become nervousness and their dynamism can turn into aggressiveness. Sometimes a Scorpio dog is unfairly considered vicious, when his unpredictable behavior really results from a lack of training in his younger days. When his Scorpio passion has been allowed to run wild, it is difficult for him to change his lifelong habits.

So be sure to give your Scorpio the guidance he needs, along with the extra helping of love that it takes to satisfy his powerful craving for affection. And then, even if he never enters a dog show, he will always take first prize in your family for his vigor and zest and for his big-hearted approach to life.

SAGITTARIUS

A Sagittarius dog is as frisky, as powerful, and as confident as the starry centaur—half man and half horse—that is the sign of this segment of the zodiac. He loves a challenge and is dependable in good times and bad. There is no better fire dog than a Sagittarius Dalmation, no better rescuer than a Sagittarius Saint Bernard.

Sagittarius dogs have a keen sense of right and wrong. They make magnificent watch dogs and, even in the home, are quick to follow commands.

Because they are so forceful—even Sagittarius pups are apt to be stronger than they look—they sometimes are impulsive. Without meaning to disobey, they will run off from home in pursuit of a rabbit or an ice-cream truck. They are also romantic animals and think nothing of spending a moonlit night howling melodies to their nearby lady love.

Sagittarians are born for the outdoors, especially for hunting. Even small breeds, Lhasa apsos and Corgis, like to stalk through garden flowers as if they were tracking down an escaped convict or finding a lost child in the woods.

Because they are so easygoing and relaxed, Sagittarius dogs find it

easy to switch masters. If their owner, for one reason or another, cannot keep them anymore and entrusts them to the care of a friend or neighbor, they readily make the adjustment and become just as devoted to their new master as they were to the former one. That experience would break the heart of many dogs; but for Sagittarius, it just means more friends and playmates.

Sagittarians like to do everything quickly, including their speech. The barking of a Sagittarius dog sometimes sounds like machine-gun fire. And for sure speed afoot, there is nothing in the canine kingdom like a Sagittarius greyhound.

There is a certain frankness and candor about a Sagittarius which takes people a while to accept. If he does not like his food or his living quarters, he will let you know it, one way or another. He does not ask much; but whatever he really wants, he will insist upon having. And in return for the few things he does need—cool water, nutritious meals, a place to run, and a warm bed in winter—he repays his master with his boisterous affection and a tail that never stops wagging.

CAPRICORN

Like their zodiac symbol — the starry goat — Capricorn dogs are agile and fleet-footed. Even a dawdling dachshund born under this sign thinks of herself as a swift greyhound.

Your Capricorn pet is alert and inquisitive. Nothing escapes her. Even when she seems to be napping, her mind is busy and her half-closed eyes are keeping track of everything happening in your household.

She is calculating and prudent. Unlike most other animals, she will deftly walk around a puddle rather than romp through it. When one gate is closed, she will waste no time barking at it but will head for the other one. She rarely chases cars, not only because it would be dangerous but also because it would waste her energy. Her concern is with more important things.

Because your Capricorn pet tends to be more serious than other dogs, she may seem haughty and aloof. This is just a sign of her personal independence. She is at her best when allowed to make her own decisions, but you can expect determined resistance when she is pulled around without her assent.

A Capricorn puppy is unusually tidy and well behaved. It is as if

she wants to be grown up before her time. She enjoys the company of adults more than games with their children, and sometimes will sit intently listening to conversation rather than play with her toys.

When she grows up, the Capricorn dog can be a model of good breeding. She and her fellow Capricorns often take first prize in dog shows. There is something royal about their self-controlled demeanor that impresses the judges as much as it pleases their happy owners.

A human Capricorn makes an excellent host, and a canine Capricorn is much the same. When guests arrive, she displays her best manners. She does not growl at the strangers or beg goodies from their plates, but sits genteelly in her place of comfort, where she can keep an eye on the proceedings.

Capricorns can be as stubborn as the goat that is their sky sign. Capricorn people make great debaters, and Capricorn dogs can take firm positions and be rigid and unyielding too. They sense when they are going to the vet for their shots and hide under the bed, refusing to even show their nose. They enjoy a brisk walk, especially if it gives them a chance to exercise their agility along slopes and across narrow bridges; but when they have had enough hiking, they simply refuse to go farther. This is a time for gentle persuasion, for Capricorns are reasonable and respond best to a cool explanation of the situation.

All dogs need affection, but a Capricorn needs respect as well. She is nobody's fool and does not like to be teased. Every so often, she retires from the bustle of everyday life to spend a few hours in seclusion, perhaps behind the sofa. This is the way all Capricorns recharge their psychic batteries, and your pet will soon come bounding back to you with new vigor and a lively interest in everything you are doing.

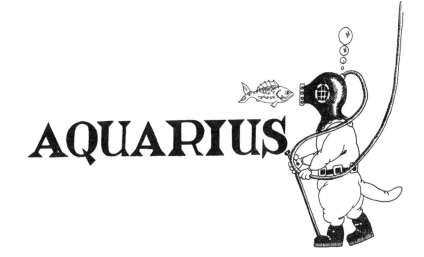

AQUARIUS

An Aquarius can be the most loving and lovable of dogs, as long as her master returns her affection. Her star sign is the heavenly Water Bearer, mild and merciful, unconventional and sensitive, changeable and sometimes fickle.

Most dogs born under this sign are as kind as Lassie. They may not show their friendship by exuberant barking, but their devotion to their owners is faithful till death. If they are abandoned, they can perish from a broken heart. When you read about a dog who keeps a silent vigil over her master's grave, chances are she is an Aquarius.

But if her owner should mistreat or ignore her, she will quickly react, either by running away or by becoming nervous and snappish. That is her way of telling the world how unhappy she is.

Because her feelings are so sensitive, she is easily hurt. She will never completely trust the neighbor who once yelled at her while she was innocently exploring his garden.

The intuition of an Aquarius dog makes her seem almost human. She will react to conversations as if she understands what is being said. She may wait in the car when you are preparing to go for a ride, or roam around the yard picking up sticks as you get ready to mow the lawn.

To her, a job well done is more important than fame. At a show, she is more interested in pleasing her master than in impressing the judge. Her affectionate nature may cause her to lick the judge's face rather than score points for her poise and reserve. She may not win his blue ribbon, but she always wins his heart.

Both the people and dogs born under the sign of Aquarius are tactful and diplomatic. Your pooch would rather walk around a canine bully than have a fight. If she has to share the household with other pets, she finds some way to keep peace with them, usually by remaining a little apart from the others. She may even carry this to extremes. If she has to mingle with many other animals or strange people, she becomes aloof and cool. When you have a party, she will retreat to the patio and refuse to socialize. Just like a shy child, she should never be forced to join the festivities.

There is an unconventional streak in all Aquarians. Your pet may have a taste for exotic foods, or she might have a favorite sitting place—under the kitchen table or in the middle of the tulip bed—right where you do not want her to be. That is the free spirit in her coming through.

Around the world, water is a symbol of life: and so it is only natural that your dog, born under the sign of the Water Bearer, should make you feel the peace and joy of life. She can show you the serenity that comes to those who find beauty in all things. But first you must show her that you cherish her and appreciate her devotion. That is the magic key that sets free the love of an Aquarius dog and of all the world as well.

PISCES

For dogs as for people, the sign of Pisces is the double fish: each of them swimming in opposite directions. That is why a Pisces, canine or human, seems to go in two ways at the same time.

Pisces dogs love to travel and make excellent companions on cross-country trips, as well as vacations into the wilderness. They are superb hiking dogs, and some of them even take to the sea as contented pets aboard sailing ships. The same trait that makes a Pisces pet a traveler can make him a roamer too. Many dogs that repeatedly wander away from home are Pisces. So if this is your dog's star sign, be sure to keep a close eye on him for his own safety.

I do not know if the first dogs sent into space aboard rockets were Pisces; but if they were, they must have enjoyed their voyage. In fact, all Pisces dogs reach for the starry heights of success. They are determined to do their best, and then some more.

Your Pisces wants to be tops, to run faster than other dogs, to win every tug of war with you over an old rope. But he tries so hard that he sometimes gets exhausted and has to lie down, panting hard, to catch his breath.

The owner of a Pisces pup has to be careful not to let the little

46

nipper hurt himself by overexertion, trying to do all the things that big dogs do. He is apt to be too confident. He thinks he can cross streets and ramble around the neighborhood without mishaps. That is why a Pisces pet needs a firm master, who will use both kindness and strength to teach him to obey.

This is very important, because even a Pisces puppy can be headstrong. If left for the night in the basement, he will strain every muscle to climb two flights of stairs so he can snuggle at the foot of his master's bed.

A Pisces pet is loyal, often to a fault. Sometimes he will not let his master alone. Just like a Pisces human, he thinks he knows what is best for everyone else. No matter whether he is a small cocker spaniel or a massive Irish wolfhound, no one takes him for a walk. He takes them! Pulling and tugging on his leash, he decides where his master will go next.

A Pisces dog is intelligent and can make a superb performer. But sometimes he is so reckless that, instead of doing tricks, he runs in circles around his trainer. That exuberance and excitement keeps a Pisces always youthful and keeps his fortunate owner always on his toes.